THE WORLD'S BIGGEST MACHINES

D1399145

Marcie Aboff

Raintree

Chicago, Illinois

www.heinemannraintree.com
Visit our website to find out
more information about
Heinemann-Raintree books.

To order:

☎ Phone 888-454-2279
💻 Visit www.heinemannraintree.com
to browse our catalog and order online.

© 2011 Raintree
an imprint of Capstone Global Library, LLC
Chicago, Illinois

Edited by Nancy Dickmann and Megan Cotugno
Designed by Jo Hinton-Malivoire
Picture research by Tracy Cummins
Production by Victoria Fitzgerald
Printed and bound in China by CTPS

14 13 12 11 10
10 9 8 7 6 5 4 3 2 1

**Library of Congress Cataloging-in-
Publication Data**
Aboff, Marcie.
  The world's biggest machines / Marcie Aboff.
    p. cm. -- (Extreme machines)
  Includes bibliographical references and index.
  ISBN 978-1-4109-3875-6 (hc) -- ISBN 978-
1-4109-3881-7 (pb) 1. Machinery--Juvenile
literature. I. Title.
  TJ147.A26 2011
  629.04'6--dc22

                    2009051227

Acknowledgments
The author and publishers are grateful to the
following for permission to reproduce copyright
material: Alamy pp. **14** (© Eric Glenn), **15** (©
INTERFOTO); AP Images p. **11** (THE CANADIAN
PRESS/Larry MacDougal); Corbis pp. **4** (© Juan
Carlos Ulate/Reuters), **6** (© Neville Elder), **13** (©
YONHAP/epa), **18** (© JOE SKIPPER/Reuters), **20** (©
BAZUKI MUHAMMAD/Reuters), **23** (© Yogi, Inc);
Getty Images pp. **12** (Munshi Ahmed/Bloomberg),
19 (Joe Raedle), **21** (Lester Lefkowitz), **22** (Time
Life Pictures); istockphoto p. **24**; Krøll Cranes A/S
p. **25**; Landov pp. **5** (DAVID GRAY/Reuters), **10**
(Norm Betts), **17** (Kyodo); Mosterlimo.com pp.
8, **9** (Bob Fisher); NASA pp. **26** (Troy Cryder), **27**;
Shutterstock p. **7** (© Michael Stokes); U.S. Navy p.
16 (Airman Natalia E. Panetta).

Cover photograph of the crawler transporter
from Kennedy Space Center, FL produced with
permission of NASA (Kennedy Space Center (NASA-
KSC).

Every effort has been made to contact copyright
holders of any material reproduced in this book.
Any omissions will be rectified in subsequent
printings if notice is given to the publisher.

Some words are shown in bold, **like this**. You can find
out what they mean by looking in the glossary.

Contents

Big Machines

Some machines are big, and others are really big. They make a car look like a toy. They carry airplanes, build tall buildings, and move rockets. If you see one coming towards you, get out of the way!

↑ Don't get caught behind these giant mining trucks!

Bigfoot Monster Truck

Bigfoot is a huge monster truck. Monster trucks are like pickup trucks. Contests are held to see which is the toughest. With tires that are 10 feet tall, Bigfoot rolls right over cars, crushing them easily.

How Big?
15.5 feet tall

EXTREME FACT
Bigfoot was the first truck to jump over a 727 jetliner!

MonsterLimo

MonsterLimo is the longest monster truck. Inside, there are leather seats, colored lights, and surround sound music. It is also high off the ground. You have to climb stairs to get in. Some cars could drive right under it!

EXTREME FACT

MonsterLimo can hold 14 passengers.

↑ MonsterLimo is stretched out!

Caterpillar 797 Truck

One of the largest haul trucks in the world is the Caterpillar 797. This powerful machine is made for big **mining** and **construction** projects. It can hold 400 tons. The tires are over 13 feet tall!

stairway and ladder

You need to climb a stairway or ladder just to get inside this truck!

How Big?
24 feet tall

128

CAT

Airbus A380

Airbus A380 is a giant jumbo jet. This fancy double-decker airplane is the largest **passenger** airplane in the world. The planes have snack bars and lounges. Some even have full size beds and showers!

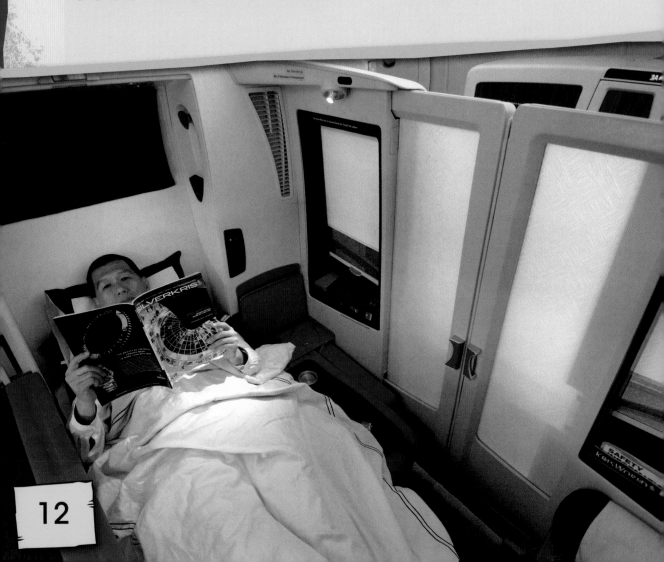

How Big?
238 feet long

EXTREME FACT
Some Airbus planes can seat 500 passengers!

Goodyear Blimp

Floating slowly across the sky, **blimps** look like huge balloons. They are filled with **helium** gas to make them float. Blimps have engines so they can be steered and **propelled.** The Goodyear blimp is one of the largest blimps flying today.

How Big?
192 feet long

Hindenburg blimp

EXTREME FACT

The biggest blimp ever created was the Hindenburg. It was 804 feet long. The Hindenburg was destroyed by fire in 1937.

Nimitz Aircraft Carrier

The U.S. Navy's Nimitz **aircraft carriers** are huge. They can hold up to 85 airplanes on their decks. They carry airplanes all over the world. Each Nimitz aircraft carrier is longer than three football fields.

EXTREME FACT

The largest Nimitz aircraft carrier weighs over 100,000 tons with a full load.

How Big?

1,092 feet long

Oasis Cruise Ship

Imagine a city floating in the middle of the ocean. That is just what cruise ship *Oasis of the Seas* feels like. This 16-deck ship carries over 6,000 **passengers**. Some Oasis cabins are as big as city apartments.

EXTREME FACT
This massive ship has a basketball court, a mini golf course, and two surfing machines!

How Big?
1,187 feet long

Container Ships

Some of the largest ships are container ships. They are used to carry goods across the ocean in large containers, or boxes. The largest of them can carry 1.3 million televisions, or 50 million cell phones!

EXTREME FACT

Despite all the weight they carry, container ships still go about 30 miles per hour (48 km/h).

How Big?

1,100 feet long

Typhoon Submarine

Russia's Typhoon **submarines** are the largest submarines in the world. The Typhoon submarines were feared for their quiet surprise attacks. Typhoon submarines can stay underwater for 120 days. They are currently used by the military for **missile** tests.

Tower Crane

How are skyscrapers built? Giant cranes help do the job! A hook hangs from the end of the crane's long arm. The hook lifts heavy objects high in the air.

hook

EXTREME FACT

This tower crane is three times as tall as the Statue of Liberty!

How Big?

Almost 1,000 feet tall

The Crawler-Transporter

One of the largest land vehicles in the world is a crawler-transporter. These machines were made for NASA. They carry rockets five miles, from the **assembly** building to the **launch pad**. They weigh 2,700 tons!

How Big?
131 feet long and 114 feet wide

EXTREME FACT

The crawler is big, but definitely not fast! It moves only one mile an hour.

3
SIDE 3

tracks

Don't get your foot caught under these tracks!

Test Yourself!

Try to match up each question with the correct answer.

① Typhoon Submarine

② Goodyear Blimp

③ Container Ship

④ Caterpillar 797

⑤ Crawler-Transporter

a Which machine transports rockets?

b Which machine can stay underwater for 120 days?

c Which machine is made for mining and construction projects?

d Which machine can carry more than a million TVs?

e Which machine is filled with helium gas?

Glossary

aircraft carrier large ship where military planes take off and land

assembly putting together of machine parts

blimp vehicle that floats through the air

construction act of building

helium a gas that is lighter than air

launch pad place where space shuttles take off

mining digging rocks out of the ground

missile a weapon for throwing or shooting

passenger person who rides in a car, truck, or other machine

propelled moved forward

submarine ship that drives underwater

Find Out More

Find out

How tall is the
Crawler-Transporter?

Books

Harrison, Paul. *Monster Trucks.*
New York: Rosen Publishing Group, 2008.

Abramson, Andra. *Ships Up Close.* New York: Sterling
Publishing, 2008.

Mugford, Simon. *Monster Machines.* New York: St. Martin's
Press, 2005.

Doeden, Matt. *Aircraft Carriers.* Minneapolis, MN: Lerner
Publishing Group, 2005.

Websites

Bigfoot Monster Trucks
http://www.bigfoot4x4.com/
Includes pictures, videos, history and more of all Bigfoot
Monster Trucks.

Typhoon Submarine
**http://channel.nationalgeographic.com/series/
break-it-down/3859/Overview**
Videos, photos, and facts about the Typhoon Submarine.

NASA
http://science.ksc.nasa.gov/facilities/crawler.html
Includes pictures and detailed information about the
Crawler-Transporter.

Index